NATIONAL
GEOGRAPHIC

PIONEER EDITION

By Sharon Katz Cooper

CONTENTS

Emperor
penguins

Penguin Parents

By Sharon Katz Cooper

Think about your family. Your parents do a lot. They buy your clothes. They cook meals. They help you with homework. They let you sit on their feet all winter to keep warm.

Wait! Your parents don't do that. But emperor penguins do. These birds live in Antarctica. It is freezing cold. Emperor penguins must work hard to keep their chicks alive.

Tough Trek

It is March in Antarctica. Fall is starting. Days are getting colder. Penguins are moving away from the sea. They are walking inland. The ice is thicker and safer there.

The penguins' journey ends a few weeks later. Some penguins have walked 70 miles. They finally get to their **rookery.** That is where they will raise their young.

EMPEROR PENGUIN PROFILE

Height: About 4 feet
Weight: 66 to 84 pounds
Food: Fish, squid, and krill
Enemies: Sea lions and killer whales
Life Span: About 20 years
Cool Trivia: Can dive 1,312 feet. That is more than the height of the Empire State Building in New York City.

Bringing Up Baby

Winter starts in June. Blinding blizzards blow in. Each mother penguin lays one egg.

The mother holds the egg on her feet. She passes the egg to the dad. They have to be careful. The chick will die if the egg touches the ice for too long.

The father places the egg in his **brood pouch.** This is a flap of skin. It keeps the egg warm.

Then the mom heads back to the sea. She must find food. She stays away for about two months. She fills up on fish. Then she comes back. She finds that her egg has hatched.

Now the mother feeds her chick. She **regurgitates** food. That means she coughs it up. The chick eats the food from its mother's mouth.

Trading Places

Now it is time for the dad to dine. He has not eaten in four months. He has lost about half of his body weight. He hurries to the sea to find food.

A few weeks pass. The dad comes back. Then the parents take turns caring for the baby. One parent babysits while the other finds food. Their work pays off. The young penguin grows bigger and stronger.

Summer finally comes. Chicks can now care for themselves. They have feathers and fat to keep them warm.

The parents head to the sea. They stay until fall. Then they walk back to the rookery to lay more eggs.

By fall, the chicks have left. In a few years, they grow up. They have babies. Their story marches on.

A Different Way of Life

Not all penguins live like emperors do. Most penguins do not risk the bitter cold. They go to warmer places in winter. They build nests where food is close.

Emperor penguins do not have an easy life. They live in the coldest place on Earth. They are tough birds. They have found ways to survive in this frozen land.

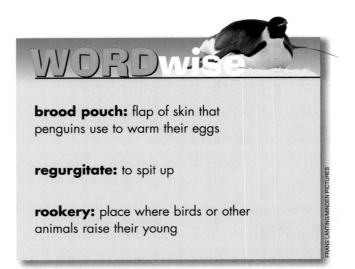

WORDwise

brood pouch: flap of skin that penguins use to warm their eggs

regurgitate: to spit up

rookery: place where birds or other animals raise their young

Super Swim

Emperor penguins are not like most birds. They are nearly four feet tall. They also cannot fly. These birds are slow on land. Yet in water, they are quick. They are born to swim. What makes these birds great swimmers? Their bodies help them survive in cold water.

1. Penguins have smooth bodies. Water moves over them easily. They are fast in water.

2. Penguins have a thick layer of fat called blubber. Blubber helps keep penguins warm.

3. Penguins have short wings called flippers. They use them like paddles as they swim.

mers

4 Penguins are covered with tiny feathers. They trap warm air and keep out the cold.

5 Body oil keeps water away from a penguin's skin. This helps a penguin stay warm.

6 A penguin has short legs and sturdy feet. They help a penguin steer in water.

Antarctica

Brrrr!
Antarctica is the land around the South Pole. It is ice cold. An ice cap covers it. That is a blanket of ice. It is two miles thick in some places. Smaller areas of ice called glaciers also cover the land. Few people live in Antarctica. Most are scientists or explorers. They stay for a while. Then they go home.

ATLANTIC OCEAN

ANTARCTIC PENINSULA

Weddell Sea

RONNE ICE SHELF

Ber Isl

Bellingshausen Sea

ELLSWORTH LAND

Vinson Massi
Highest elevation in Antarctica (16,06.

WEST ANTARCT

Amundsen Sea

MARIE BYRD LA

◀ Few people have ever climbed Antarctica's mountains. This one is called "The Razor." It is near the coast in Queen Maud Land.

Land Regions: Mountains divide the land into two parts. The east is mostly flat. The west has mountains.

Water: Most of the fresh water on Earth is in Antarctica. The water is frozen in the ice caps.

Climate: Antarctica is windy and dry. It gets little snow. Most of the snow that falls turns to ice.

Plants: Billions of tiny plants live in the oceans. A few kinds of small plants grow on the land.

Animals: Penguins and other birds nest on the coast. Whales and seals live in the oceans.

PACIFI OCEA

◀ Sea

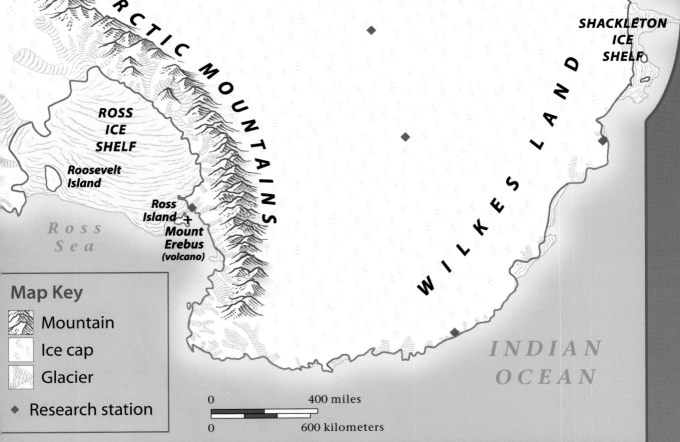

INDIAN
OCEAN

QUEEN MAUD LAND

ENDERBY
LAND

ANTARCTICA

+ South Pole

EAST ANTARCTICA

TRANSANTARCTIC MOUNTAINS

SHACKLETON
ICE
SHELF

ROSS
ICE
SHELF

WILKES LAND

Roosevelt
Island

Ross
Island +
Mount
Erebus
(volcano)

Ross
Sea

INDIAN
OCEAN

Map Key

Mountain

Ice cap

Glacier

◆ Research station

0   400 miles

0   600 kilometers

Poles Apart

The North Pole and South Pole have a lot in common. Both are very cold. Both are covered with ice. Yet these two places have many differences.

The North Pole is in the Arctic Ocean. Many groups of people live near the North Pole. So do reindeer and polar bears. Winter begins in December. Temperatures go as low as −32°F.

The South Pole is in Antarctica. This is icy land. It is surrounded by water. Not many people live near the South Pole. Penguins are some of the few animals that call Antarctica home. Winter begins in June. Temperatures go lower than −100°F!

Coldest −32°F

ALASKA
RUSSIA
CANADA
GREENLAND

DEC. 1 WINTER

2 miles

JUNE 1 WINTER

17 ft
16 ft
15 ft
14 ft

Coldest −129°F

LORI OSIECKI

Where Are You?

Read each sentence. Does the clue point to the North Pole or the South Pole? Or could you be in either place?

1 You discover penguin feathers stuck in ice.

2 You see a volcano in in the distance.

3 A native friend gives you a pair of mukluks (shoes made of reindeer skin).

4 The thermometer reads −128°F.

5 You find some polar bear footprints.

6 A huge iceberg floats by. It is a chunk of ice.

7 You come across a beached whale.

8 You hear seal barks.

Penguins

It is time to dive in and see what you have learned about penguins.

1 Why do emperor penguins keep eggs on their feet?

2 Why do mothers leave their eggs?

3 How do penguin parents raise their young?

4 What makes emperor penguins great swimmers?

5 How are Antarctica and the Arctic alike? How are they different?